DELHI
THE CITY AT A GLANC

British Council
Hidden among the shops and off
on Kasturba Gandhi Marg, Charl(
simple yet striking British Counci
is one of Delhi's modern architectural gems.
See p070

Jawahar Vyapar Bhawan
Looking like it was built out of Meccano, this
cantilevered red and yellow sandstone tower
is one of Delhi's tallest office blocks and
home to its largest handicrafts emporium.
See p064

The Imperial
A gleaming white cube of early colonial
modernism, the Imperial is hands down Delhi's
best-looking hotel. Rooms straight out of the
Raj, and service a maharaja couldn't fault.
See p026

Jantar Mantar
Part alien artefact, part architectural whimsy,
what appears at first to be a collection of
abstract red sandstone sculptures is in fact the
remains of an 18th-century royal observatory.
See p010

India Gate
At the centre of a web of busy roads, India's
largest war memorial looks like it once stood
on the Champs-Élysées and offers superb
night views of Rashtrapati Bhawan (see p066).
See p013

Rajpath
This broad, garden-lined processional
avenue, so popular with evening strollers,
links India Gate to the seat of government,
and was once the axis of imperial New Delhi.

INTRODUCTION
THE CHANGING FACE OF THE URBAN SCENE

India's sprawling capital seems to have a hole in its heart – just where you'd expect the densest urbanisation you find an anti-urban leafy core. This is due to two events that occurred within decades of each other. The first was the decision in 1911 by the country's then British rulers to create their own imperial capital, New Delhi – a purpose-built garden city located on the southern outskirts of the old Moghul city. The second was the partition of India in 1947, and the mass transfer of millions of people. Delhi was flooded with Hindu and Sikh refugees from Pakistan, doubling its population overnight. Many ended up staying, surrounding the old and new cities with hastily built neighbourhoods.

The centre of India's cultural and political gravity, today's Delhi is home to artists, writers, civil servants and politicians. At the same time, it is a place of excess. The old money blames Delhi's Punjabis, who they portray as brash, bustling and nouveau, though without them the city would have considerably less fizz, not to mention fewer restaurants, nightspots and shopping malls.

Like the rest of India, Delhi is furiously upgrading itself. New roads, flyovers and a metro system are under construction for the 2010 Commonwealth Games, giving the city the appearance of a giant building site. Yet despite this, and the dust clouds it creates, the overriding impression Delhi creates is of a green, stately city, attributes of which its 14 million inhabitants are fiercely proud.

ESSENTIAL INFO
FACTS, FIGURES AND USEFUL ADDRESSES

TOURIST OFFICE
88 Janpath
Connaught Place
T 011 2332 0005
www.delhitourism.nic.in

TRANSPORT
Car hire
Avis
Indira Gandhi International Airport
T 011 2565 4082
www.avis.com
Taxis
Asian Taxi
Lodi Road
T 011 2461 7665

EMERGENCY SERVICES
Ambulance
T 102
Fire
T 101
Police
T 100
24-hour pharmacy
Chemico
Opposite Marina Hotel
H-45
Connaught Place
T 011 2332 1874

EMBASSIES
British High Commission
Shantipath
Chanakyapuri
T 011 2687 2161
www.britishhighcommission.gov.uk
US Embassy
Shantipath
Chanakyapuri
T 011 2419 8000
newdelhi.usembassy.gov

MONEY
American Express
Hamilton House, Connaught Place
T 012 4280 1800

POSTAL SERVICES
Post Office
Dak Bhawan
Parliament Street
T 011 2309 6076
Shipping
UPS
D-12/1 Okhla Industrial Area Phase II
T 011 2638 9323

BOOKS
Bernier's Travels in the Mogul Empire
by François Bernier (Ross & Perry)
City of Djinns: A Year in Delhi
by William Dalrymple (Flamingo)
Imperial Delhi: The British Capital of the Indian Empire by Andreas Volwahsen (Prestel)

WEBSITES
Architecture
forum.indianarchitecture.net
Newspaper
timesofindia.indiatimes.com

COST OF LIVING
Taxi from Indira Gandhi International Airport to Connaught Place
£3.50
Cappuccino
£0.40
Packet of cigarettes
£1.20
Daily newspaper
£0.05
Bottle of champagne
£55

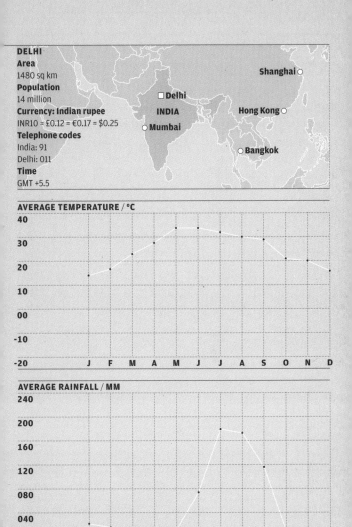

DELHI
Area
1480 sq km
Population
14 million
Currency: Indian rupee
INR10 = £0.12 = €0.17 = $0.25
Telephone codes
India: 91
Delhi: 011
Time
GMT +5.5

Shanghai ○

Delhi □
INDIA

Hong Kong ○

Mumbai ○

Bangkok ○

AVERAGE TEMPERATURE / °C

	40											
	30											
	20											
	10											
	00											
	-10											
	-20	J	F	M	A	M	J	J	A	S	O	N	D

AVERAGE RAINFALL / MM

	240											
	200											
	160											
	120											
	080											
	040											
	000	J	F	M	A	M	J	J	A	S	O	N	D

NEIGHBOURHOODS
THE AREAS YOU NEED TO KNOW AND WHY

To help you navigate the city, we've chosen the most interesting districts (see below and the map inside the back cover) and colour-coded our featured venues, according to their location; those venues that are outside these areas are not coloured.

OLD DELHI

One hundred years ago, the walled city was Delhi – the imperial capital of 17th-century Moghul emperor Shah Jahan – famous for its richly decorated mansions and splendid public buildings. Echoes of its courtly life still reverberate through India's culture and cuisine, though today Old Delhi is a shadow of its former self. Many mansions were subdivided, and while some beautiful buildings remain, the area is better known as India's largest wholesale market.

CONNAUGHT PLACE

The city's former hub has fallen out of favour in recent years, as Delhi's centre has moved decisively south. But it is still popular with tourists, who are drawn by the Jantar Mantar observatory (see p010), the plethora of state handicrafts emporia and The Imperial hotel (see p026), a colonial gem. The streets to the south of the hotel are lined with one of the few concentrations of high-rises in the city.

INDIA GATE

This is the heart of Sir Edwin Lutyens' New Delhi. The cluster of imposing government buildings that he designed around India Gate must surely rate as among the most magnificent in the world. In particular, the perspective along the Rajpath, the processional way linking India Gate to the Secretariat, is jaw-dropping. By the time these buildings were finished, India was well on its way to independence.

CHANAKYAPURI

One of Delhi's newer districts, this area is dominated by embassies and the large hotels that service them. Constructed at a time when Delhi was a prestigious posting, the embassies provide some of the finest examples of mid-century modernism in the city, including Edward D Stone's glorious American Embassy (Shantipath, T 2419 8000) and the fabulously Stalinist Russian Embassy (Shantipath, T 2687 3802). Broad avenues ensure traffic is never a problem.

LODI AND NIZAMUDDIN

Its leafy boulevards and extensive parks make Lodi one of the most sought-after parts of town. The area is characterised by Joseph Allen Stein's modernist structures, located along Max Mueller Marg, and by Lutyens' whitewashed bungalows. Nearby Nizamuddin is an exercise in contrast. A pocket of Old Delhi, it is poor, crumbling and decrepit, but home to some exquisite Moghul mosques and tombs of Sufi saints.

SOUTH DELHI

This district is a mix of private residential colonies – India's decades-old equivalent of the gated community – government housing estates, massive clusters of new shopping malls and always-busy highways. Less green and more crowded than the likes of Lodi, this new New Delhi is where much of the city's business class settle and where many of the more interesting shops and restaurants can be found.

LANDMARKS

THE SHAPE OF THE CITY SKYLINE

Rome was built on seven hills. Delhi is commonly said to have been built on seven cities, although sticklers would probably place that figure closer to 16. Either way, it has had many incarnations. Few of them carried the city's name, and many left little behind. Of Indraprastha, the first proto-Delhi, only pottery shards remain, as the site was reused by 16th-century Moghul emperor Humayun for his citadel and is now home to the exquisite remains of Purana Qila (off Mathura Road). Others left a visible imprint too, mostly religious buildings, tombs and palaces. Safdarjung (Aurobindo Marg), Lodi Garden (see p092), Qutab Minar (see p012), the historic structures on Chandni Chowk (see p014) – the relics of Delhi's past are scattered all over.

The bigger sites are wrapped in a protective belt of park, though most have simply been swallowed up by the city's growth. In a few whimsical cases, such as the Sabz Burj (Dr Zakir Hussain Marg), they have become the centrepiece of traffic roundabouts. The 'graveyard of empires' or, as Lord Curzon once called it, the 'dead seat of Muslim kings', Delhi has always been known for its architectural bones. Curzon thought the new capital a colossal waste of money and vehemently opposed it, but wasn't ultimately able to do more than object. In that, we are fortunate, for it was the British who left Delhi some of the most impressive bones of all. *For full addresses, see Resources.*

Jantar Mantar

This extraordinary site is all that remains of the observatory of Jai Singh, the Maharaja of Jaipur. Built in 1724, these abstract structures made of marble and sandstone seem resolutely contemporary, a massive art installation perhaps, or the toys of a giant child. Most were designed for solar observation. The Samrat Yantra (right), with its giant triangular central staircase, is effectively a sundial. Right next to it, the Misra Yantra, with its twin curving staircases and a central stairway, is for measuring the positions of celestial bodies. Elsewhere, the Ram Yantra was used for reading vertical and horizontal angles, and the twin hemispheres of the Jai Prakash for determining the position of the stars. The plethora of tall buildings around the site, such as the unfinished hulking concrete NDDC Convention Hall, make accurate readings impossible today.
Sansad Marg, www.jantarmantar.org

Qutab Minar

Begun in 1202 and probably finished around 30 years later, this extraordinary red sandstone tower was said to link the earth to heaven. The 72.5m structure has a rather disproportionate bulge to its lower levels, but it is easy to appreciate the awe it must have inspired at the time. Fluted and divided into five sections by filigreed balconies, the heavily carved surface is a synthesis of Indian decorative elements and inscriptions of Koranic verses. It seems to have been built more to commemorate the Moghul victory over the Rajputs than as a minaret, for which it was simply too high. The top was destroyed by lightning in 1368 and replaced by two smaller sections, built mostly from white marble. The base of the even larger but never-completed Alai Minar is located a little to the north. *Mehrauli*

India Gate

Adding a pinch of Paris to New Delhi, India Gate stands at the eastern end of the Rajpath, which leads to Rashtrapati Bhavan, the building originally intended to house parliament. Designed by Sir Edwin Lutyens and finished in 1921, the 42m-high freestanding arch, which is dramatically lit at night, began life with the less snappy name of the All-India War Memorial. It was built to commemorate the 90,000 Indian soldiers who died in WWI, and their names are etched along the walls of the arch. In 1971, India added its own touch with the installation of an eternal flame to honour *Amar Jawan*, the Immortal Soldier. Behind the gate is a sandstone *chatri*, a canopied stand, which originally housed a statue of King George V. It was removed in 1968, and today the *chatri* stands empty.
Rajpath

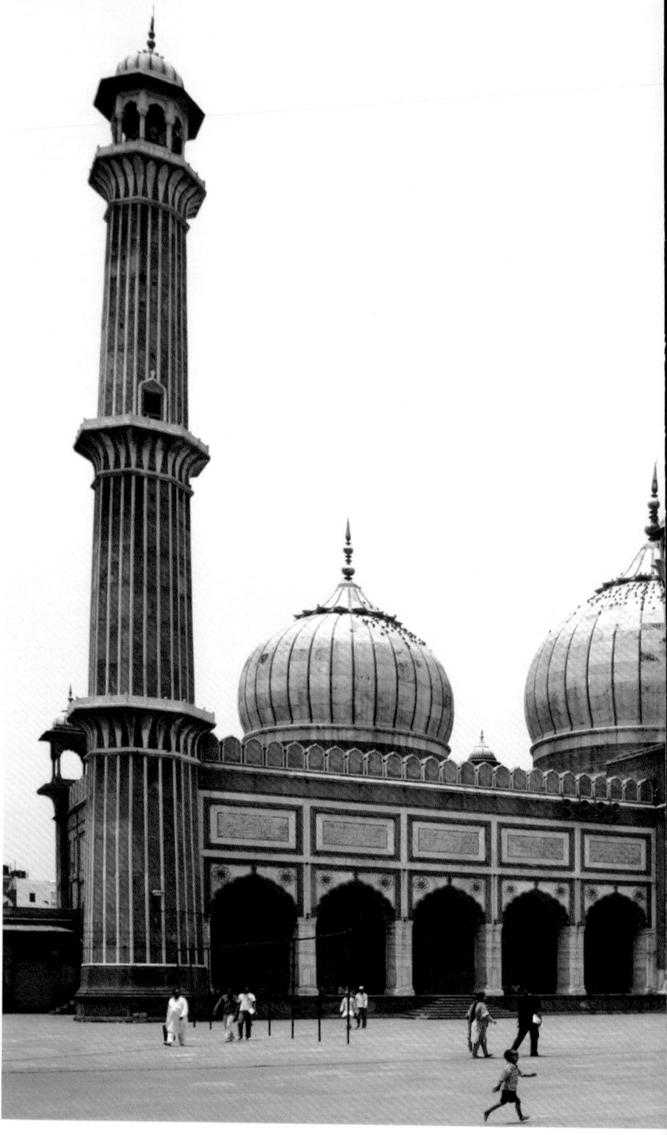

Jama Masjid

Built by Shah Jahan as the mosque for Friday prayers, the 17th-century Jama Masjid is one of the jewels of Old Delhi. The domes are clad in white marble, but the main prayer hall and the delicate open arcades are carved out of a pink-red sandstone that gradually changes hue throughout the day, from a dun colour at noon to a deep rose at sunset. *Chandni Chowk*

HOTELS

WHERE TO STAY AND WHICH ROOMS TO BOOK

Considering it's the capital of one of the world's largest countries, Delhi is dismally short on decent hotels. Of the 155 or so listed in the tourism brochures, only a handful are worthy of consideration and fewer still are in good condition. As a result, finding a room can be an exercise in frustration. Hotels like The Imperial (see po26) and The Oberoi (see po20) are regularly block-booked by tour groups, so it's best to plan as far ahead as possible, and even then don't assume that you will get the room you want.

The logical solution would be to build more hotels, but given the exorbitant land prices, height restrictions and stringent zoning laws, most new ventures have been forced out to Delhi's fringes, especially the satellite city of Gurgaon in the neighbouring state of Haryana. The sole exception is a new Amanresort currently under construction off Lodi Road. A 60-room boutique property with all Aman's signature flourishes, it's due for completion by 2009-2010. At the moment, Gurgaon is too far out to be convenient for most visitors, especially when ferocious traffic jams routinely turn the trip into Delhi into a gruelling hour-and-a-half slog. That said, once the new underground system comes into play in 2010, the journey will be more manageable. By then, a Four Seasons should be open, but should you opt for Gurgaon meanwhile, the opulent Trident Hilton (see po28) is definitely the best bet.
For full addresses and room rates, see Resources.

The Claridges

A white horseshoe-shaped post-deco box wrapped around a manicured lawn, The Claridges (no relation to the London hotel) could not be better located. A sprawling property, built wing by wing, it was one of the grandest addresses in town during its heyday, with maharajas on its guest list. The décor, as in the lobby (overleaf), falls somewhere between colonial charm and 1950s farmhouse but, as with many of Delhi's top-end hotels, it is in the midst of a renovation. Like The Imperial (see p026), The Claridges went through a dark period, recovering only after an initial makeover in 2002. The aim, ultimately, is to transform it into a boutique hotel with a contemporary feel – in the meantime, book yourself into one of the Deluxe Rooms (above).
12 Aurangzeb Road, T 011 4133 5133, www.claridges-hotels.com

Lobby, The Claridges

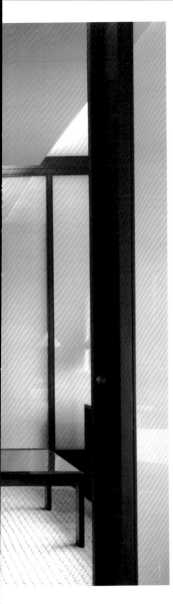

The Oberoi

Years of piecemeal renovation have left The Oberoi without a uniform identity. The asymmetrical pool could be Palm Springs circa 1960; the lobby, with its black marble and gold detailing, is more LA 1980s; and the rest of the building is caught at various points between the 1960s and the modern day. Having settled on a contemporary aesthetic – epitomised by the spectacular Virgile and Stone-designed spa (see p094) and restaurants Threesixty° (see p039) and Travertino (see p042) – The Oberoi is now undergoing an overhaul. The 334 sq m Kohinoor Suite (left) is delightful, but many of the rooms have not yet been tackled and look frumpy. Don't let this put you off: the staff are impeccably polite, the service is seamless and each room has a view, over Delhi Golf Club or Humayun's Tomb. The Oberoi is the very best of the chain hotels. *Dr Zakir Hussain Marg, T 011 2436 3030, www.oberoidelhi.com*

Maidens Hotel

For a long time, the Maidens was Delhi's only Western-style hotel of repute, and it is practically the only one worth considering this far to the north. Former guests include Lutyens, who stayed here when he came to design the capital. Today, it has fallen on hard times; despite its purchase by The Oberoi group, it's not of the same standard as its sister property (see p020), although renovations are underway. Rooms, such as the Luxury Suite (above), can feel rather cold, an impression heightened by the soaring ceilings. From the outside, though, it remains magnificent, a Georgian mansion overlooking the Red Fort (see p034) and the Jama Masjid (see p014). Atmospheric in that crumbling ghosts-of-the-Raj way India does so well, Maidens is perfect for a day or two if you want to see the old city. *7 Sham Nath Marg, T 011 2397 5464*

The Park

With hot pink and powder-blue furniture, mood lighting, beaded curtain walls and Sanskrit characters carved into the walls of the corridors – the décor is courtesy of London's Conran & Partners – The Park is the city's foremost design hotel. It has also become a favourite watering hole of Delhi's bright young things, who come to flirt and make merry in the dramatic bar or to lounge after a buffet lunch on the deck around the small but perfectly formed pool. Equally bijou is the hotel's revamped spa. The rooms are well appointed with all mod cons, and the suites on The Residence floors, such as the Presidential (above), have their own sitting room (overleaf) and access to a business centre and club area. The hotel's vibe is playful; naughty but nice.
15 Parliament Street, T 011 2374 3000, newdelhi.theparkhotels.com

Living Room, Presidential Suite, The Park

The Imperial

Set in acres of gardens right in the heart of the city, this gorgeous example of early colonial modernism, with its jasmine-scented halls and its opulent interiors, is hands down the best hotel in town. After a rough patch in the 1980s, when it briefly became a backpackers' hostel, The Imperial has recovered spectacularly. In 2002, it was given an overhaul, the potted palms and Persian rug aesthetic subtly updated with the addition of massive flower sculptures and modern amenities like wi-fi. With the exception of the 195 sq m Royal Imperial Suite (right), which comes with a jacuzzi and a steam room, a study and a butler's pantry, rooms are a little snug, but they do come with a walk-in closet. Reserve one facing the gardens (150 has a great view of the pool) and indulge your *Passage to India* fantasies.
Janpath, T 011 2334 1234, theimperialindia.com

Trident Hilton

Though it is awkwardly located for those interested in Delhi's historical sights, the Trident lies at the centre of one of the capital's most rapidly expanding satellite zones. From the imposing entrance, with its water features and burning braziers, to the tasteful and well-appointed rooms, such as the Deluxe (right), and its enticing pool (above), the Trident is an oasis of tranquillity in the chaos that is Gurgaon. As famous, at the moment, for its traffic jams and the clouds of dust kicked up by work on the new metro, road expansions and a building frenzy that makes Dubai look anaemic, Gurgaon is home to Delhi's IT and media industries and an increasing proportion of its more upwardly mobile citizens. The new malls, multiplexes and bars and restaurants attract huge crowds of non-residents, especially at weekends.
443 Udyog Vihar, Gurgaon, T 012 4245 0505, www.trident-hilton.com

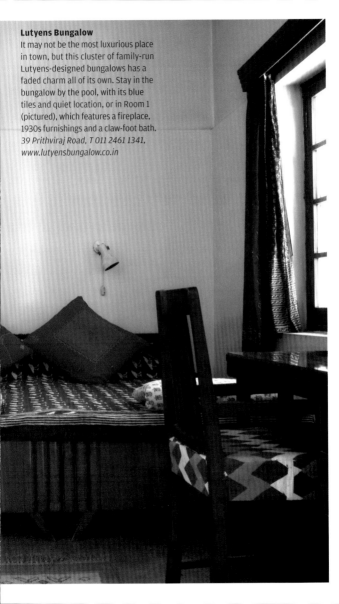

Lutyens Bungalow
It may not be the most luxurious place in town, but this cluster of family-run Lutyens-designed bungalows has a faded charm all of its own. Stay in the bungalow by the pool, with its blue tiles and quiet location, or in Room 1 (pictured), which features a fireplace, 1930s furnishings and a claw-foot bath.
39 Prithviraj Road, T 011 2461 1341, www.lutyensbungalow.co.in

24 HOURS

SEE THE BEST OF THE CITY IN JUST ONE DAY

Make the most of your day in Delhi by starting early, as traffic snarls can add hours to even short journeys. Then there is the weather. Summers – late March until the end of November, with the monsoon in the middle – are intense. By 11am, the mercury will have already hit 40°C, so you won't want to be outside.

Begin at about 8am with a stroll along the river through the park at Raj Ghat (opposite). From there, head north, skirting the old city walls, to Maidens Hotel (see p022) for breakfast on the lawn. Suitably fortified, plunge back into the chaos of crumbling Old Delhi and spend a few hours at the Red Fort (see p034), the most beautiful Moghul building after the Taj Mahal. Exit via Chandni Chowk and then walk or take a cab to Connaught Place.

Pause for lunch at Veda (see p036), and afterwards, if you don't fancy doing as the locals do and taking an afternoon nap, try the refurbished 1930s Rivoli Cinema (Baba Kharak Singh Marg, T 011 4150 2782) for a Bollywood matinee or The Imperial (see p026) for afternoon tea in the jasmine-scented Atrium.

Next, visit the Nature Morte gallery (see p038), to discover work by the rising stars of India's art scene, before heading to Nizamuddin as the sun sets for a stroll through the gardens at Humayun's Tomb (Mathura Road). End your day with a cocktail and dinner at The Oberoi's ultra-modern Threesixty° (see p039). *For full addresses, see Resources.*

08.00 Raj Ghat

An early morning stroll in this park along the Yamuna River as the mist begins to dissipate is one of Delhi's least known but perhaps most enjoyable pleasures. Come too late, on national holidays or over the weekend, and you may find yourself sharing your walk with coachloads of Indian tourists and devotees of Mahatma Gandhi, who come to lay flowers at the black marble platform (above) that marks the site where he was cremated. Memorials to other Indian political notables can also be seen here – Indira Gandhi's is a grey-red monolith and her son Rajiv's is a large stone lotus blossom surrounded by 46 small blooms, one for each year of his life. Nehru's cremation site, Shantivan (The Forest of Peace), is particularly beautiful, set in lovingly landscaped surroundings. *Mahatma Gandhi Marg*

11.00 Red Fort
Of all Old Delhi's marvels, the Red Fort,
or Lal Qila, is easily the most magnificent.
Built by Shah Jahan in the 17th century,
it was designed as a city-within-a-city
rather than a mere defensive structure.
Once home to more than 3,000 people,
the fort contained an army barracks
and the royal palace, and everything
associated with it, from kitchens and
stables to hammams (left), a harem,
reception halls, audience chambers and
a mosque. Though the fort was altered
by the British after they put down the
1857 uprising, there is still a sense of its
original glory. Inside the 33m-high walls,
the lavishly decorated Mumtaz Mahal
(now an archaeological museum) and the
Diwan-i-Khas, or Hall of Private Audience,
are guaranteed to entrance, while the
emperor's legendary pleasure gardens
are a perfect respite from the hectic city.
Netaji Subhash Marg

13.30 Veda

Among Connaught Place's booksellers,
kitchen appliance shops and showrooms
still bearing imperial seals of approval,
Veda's interior is a bold collision between
Marbella 1976 and Moghul mirror palace.
Veda began life as a 'fusion' restaurant,
combining classic Indian and other
Asian flavours, but it was a step too far
for Delhi's foodies. A reversion to much
simpler, northern Indian fare served with
a contemporary twist, such as pyramids
of rice and cone-shaped poppadoms, for
example, resurrected its appeal. Expect
tandoori, kebabs, plenty of paneer and
more unusual treats, such as lotus-root
crisps. With its leather banquettes,
orange walls and red glass chandeliers,
Veda comes into its own after dark, but
is nevertheless a pleasant place to escape
the searing early afternoon heat.
H-27 Outer Circle, T 011 4151 3535

16.00 Nature Morte

Walk into this space in a 1960s villa set on a leafy street and you could be forgiven for thinking you were in New York. Peter Nagy's itinerant gallery, which has had a variety of homes since it opened in 1997, is a reincarnation of the space of the same name that he and Alan Belcher ran in the East Village in the 1980s. Focused primarily on photography, installation and conceptual art, Nature Morte has gained a reputation for showcasing some of India's most challenging and experimental works by emerging and mid-level artists, such as Arun Kumar, Bharti Kher, Mithu Sen and Ranbir Kaleka. With its vigorous schedule of exhibitions, this innovative gallery can be counted on to have something worth going to see almost every day of the year. *A-1 Neeti Bagh, T 011 4174 0215, www.naturemorte.com*

20.00 Threesixty°

The Oberoi hotel's restaurant is, hands down, Delhi's most visually impressive dining experience. Famous for its sushi, Threesixty° also serves an eclectic menu of international offerings. At lunchtime, there is a buffet feast favoured by hotel guests, but come evening the atmosphere changes completely, with low lighting and intimate seating attracting a good-looking crowd of sophisticated Delhi-ites. Though altogether less formal than The Oberoi's other restaurant, Travertino (see p042), it's best to make an effort if you'd rather not spend the evening being subjected to mildly disapproving stares.

The Oberoi, Dr Zakir Hussain Marg,
T 011 2436 3030, www.oberoidelhi.com

URBAN LIFE
CAFÉS, RESTAURANTS, BARS AND NIGHTCLUBS

Roadside *dhabas* and cafeteria-style eateries aside, until recently there was no real dining culture in Delhi. When people wanted 'something special', they went to a hotel. Over the last five years, stand-alone restaurants have proliferated, but the sky-high land prices and rigid zoning regulations have forced most to open in odd locations. Fickle customers and even more fickle municipal authorities mean design is not a priority. Nearly all the best places to eat – if you want Indian, anyway – are the least attractive.

The fabulous south Indian thalis at Andhra Bhavan (1 Ashoka Marg, 011 2338 7499), the Bengali delights at Oh! Calcutta (HS-1 International Trade Tower, Nehru Place, 011 2646 4180) and street treats like the *bedmi aloo* at Mohan Ram (off Gali Parethwali) are mouthwatering but the eateries are visually unappealing. This creates a dilemma. Go for good food or a good-looking restaurant? Delhi's élite opts for the latter, showing an increasing preference for European, Asian fusion or Leb-iterranean rather than Indian.

Think of this list as representing the first wave. Contemporary design has arrived with a vengeance, although the tendency is still to copy. The food is more inventive but consistency varies, even at the better restaurants. The background music? Well, that's always the same lounge tracks. Still, Delhi has come a long way and, as diners become more demanding, things can only improve. *For full addresses, see Resources.*

Agni

If the chic uniforms, the geometric white tiles and the clean lines of the furnishings are emphatically international, courtesy of Conran & Partners, the menu at Agni leaves you in absolutely no doubt where you are. Perhaps Delhi's most successful experiment with contemporary Indian cuisine, the kitchen at Agni serves classic dishes from all over the subcontinent, but the emphasis on organic produce and a light touch with both butter and spices gives even the most familiar dishes new life. Desserts are a particular speciality; whatever else you order from the menu, do not miss out on the chocolate *jamun* or the *paan ki rasmalai*, a light creamy dessert flavoured with pistachio, saffron and a sprinkling of chopped *paan* leaves.
Park Hotel, 15 Parliament Street,
T 011 2347 3000

Travertino

With its classic contemporary furniture, backlit panels of translucent travertine and walk-through glass box of a wine cellar at the entrance, Travertino is an undertaking in understated elegance, thanks to the British-based designers Virgile and Stone. This also extends to the plate – ravioli of tuna; gnocchi with buffalo mozzarella; black truffles and grilled vegetables in balsamic vinegar.

Head chef Tommaso Maddalena's classic Italian dishes, some entirely of his own invention, are all superbly executed, and all served with a twist that makes them distinctively Travertino. The desserts are sublime, as are the cheeses, several of them regional specialities with which many diners will not be familiar.
The Oberoi, Dr Zakir Hussain Marg,
T 011 2436 3030

Jade

Most hotels in Delhi boast an oriental outlet of some variety – one even had an entire *sushi-ya* sent from Japan and reassembled in the basement. Jade moves to the beat of a different drum. Eschewing the trend towards fusion of every flavour, it offers solid Szechuan fare, with the sole concession to culinary gymnastics being the separate *yum cha* menu, offering 40 kinds of dim sum. Jade is timeless in that almost ubiquitous contemporary Asian way: an entrance with dark-wood screens concealing a host of jade ornaments, windows looking onto bamboo trees, padded fabric walls, gold-foil ceiling and red lacquer details and modern furniture. Blissfully quiet by day, this bijou is a delicious city-centre getaway. *The Claridges, 12 Aurangzeb Road, T 011 4133 5133, www.claridges-hotels.com*

Olive Beach

Maybe it's the setting, maybe it's the menu, featuring what is universally agreed to be the tastiest Mediterranean food in town, but ever since its original incarnation in a merchant's house in Old Delhi (this first location was a victim of Delhi municipality's zoning laws), Olive Beach (formerly Olive Bar and Kitchen) has drawn a glamorous crowd. Now part of Hotel Diplomat, it is as popular with the city's culturati as it is with visiting Bollywood royalty, fashion designers and Delhi's better-dressed media moguls (whose one goal often appears to be trying to out-drink one another). Be it the food, the cocktails or the chance to see and be seen, Olive Beach continues to be a great success.

Hotel Diplomat, Diplomatic Enclave, 9 Sadar Patel Marg, T 011 2664 2552

Ploof!

Placing a heavy emphasis on seafood, which is not easy to come by in landlocked Delhi, Ploof! sources its salmon from Norway, its lobsters from Phuket and its baby octopuses from Japan. The menu is a mixture of Creole, Mediterranean and South-East Asian flavours – some, like the Malaysian yellow curry, more authentic than others. A consistent favourite is the sea bass in Goan masala. If none of the dishes appeal, you can choose your own fish and have it prepared the way you like. The simple interior – think contemporary colonial casual – makes this a perfect escape from the heat and dust. Close your eyes as you savour your Death by Chocolate, and you could almost be on the veranda of a Portuguese house in Panaji.
13 Lodi Colony Main Market,
T 011 2464 9026

Magique

Food writer Marut Sikka's stylish venture is an essay in Asian fusion, which is odd, given his expertise in Indian food. That quibble aside, Sikka's restaurant, which is open for dinner only, often lives up to its unabashedly cornball name. The menu, best perused over a wasabi martini, has some real winners; tandoori lemongrass chicken for one, as well as the sumptuous duck in tamarind sauce, a combination of flavours and textures certain to please the pickiest diner. A little inconveniently located, this is one of the few places in Delhi where it is both possible and pleasurable to eat outdoors, though the cool interior, with its dark woods, rustic furnishings and black-and-white photos of India, is a pleasant alternative.
Gate 3, Garden of Five Senses, Saidulajab, T 011 2953 6767

Fire

From the bar staff decked out in costumes by Indian fashion designer Rohit Bal to the dark-wood bar, backlit to resemble molten metal, Fire is every bit as design-oriented as its more demure sister, Agni (see p041), next door. Whether you choose to stand at the bar, reserve one of the glowing glass tables and sink into a soft leather tub-chair, or lounge amid the golden velvet cushions on the massive leather divans in front of the dramatic orange light wall, you'll see that Fire attracts an immaculately groomed crowd of the young and (very) beautiful – not to mention the nabobs who lust after them. As the dancefloor gets crowded and scruples lubricated, don't be surprised if things begin to get devilishly hot.
Park Hotel, 15 Parliament Street,
T 011 2347 3000, www.theparkhotels.com

Smoke House Grill

As the name implies, Smoke House, tucked away down an unassuming side street, is devoted to all things smoked. Everything, whether it's meat, fish, cheese or even fruit, like the apple in the apple martini, is smoked on the premises. Downstairs, there's a lively atmosphere among the manga-print panels and backlit silk walls, and the suspended tables to one side of the bar are particularly in demand. Upstairs, the mood is calmer, with cooler colours and more formal table settings, in addition to a semi-private dining area. Start with smoked tomato and lemongrass soup, then head straight for the breaded John Dory, served on a bed of creamy leeks. Round off with a post-dinner digestif and consider the merits of buying your own smoke oven. *2 North Wing, Vipps Centre, Greater Kailash, T 011 4143 5530*

Aura

There is something distinctly Sherman McCoy about Aura. Perhaps it's the red neon uplighters fringing the ceiling, the charcoal tones or the stainless-steel and black leather bar stools, but the overall effect has a definite whiff of Master of the Universe about it. In a city with few respectable bars, as opposed to bars that are also restaurants, this is one spot that is unabashedly dedicated to liquid sustenance – the harder, the better. The array of Scotches, gins and so on is supplemented by the widest selection of vodkas in Delhi, more than 60 in all, many of which are impossible to find elsewhere.
The Claridges, 12 Aurangzeb Marg,
T 011 4133 5133, www.claridges-hotels.com

Ivy

Red crystal chandeliers and dark-wood ceiling aside, Ivy is essentially an exercise in off-whites, hence the cream-coloured panelled walls, the crisp linen tablecloths and the ivory fabric on the bar stools and chairs. The narrow entrance opens onto a double-height dining area, longer than it is wide, with one wall occupied by an illuminated bar and the other by a room-length bench. The raised lounge area is perfect for those who are here to be seen, and the dining area is ideal for those who like to watch them. As the rows of bottles artfully displayed above the bar attest, Ivy is oriented to the after-dark crowd, but that should not detract from the food. The menu is decidedly international – highlights include porcini tartlets, rack of New Zealand lamb and grilled salmon with skordalia potatoes – and the portions are generous.
Lotus Tower, New Friends Colony,
T 011 4162 7744

INSIDER'S GUIDE

APARNA CHANDRA, FASHION DESIGNER

A diehard Delhi-ite, stylist and fashion designer Aparna Chandra says she loves her home town for its 'architecture and culture, its greenery and chaos, its people and the exciting time it's going through'. A haggler at heart, she is enchanted by Delhi's bazaars: Paharganj (Chelmsford Road) is her favourite stop for clothing, belts, Buddha statues and 'the best hummus this side of Beirut'. For trinkets and 'the most spectacular *chana*', she goes to the Tuesday Market at the Hanuman Temple (Baba Kharak Singh Marg). For street food, she visits Bengali Market (Tansen Marg).

She likes the Italian eaterie Flavors (49-54 C Moolchand Flyover Complex, Defence Colony, T 011 2464 5644) for its outdoor setting and relaxed vibe, but for something sophisticated, Chandra will head to either Olive Beach (see p045), which is known for its glam crowd and delicious Mediterranean food, or Magique (see p047), which she appreciates as much for the chance to stroll in the gardens as she does the opportunity to eat alfresco on the terrace.

After hours generally means hanging out in Shalom (18 N Block Market, Greater Kailash, T 011 4163 2280), a lounge and shisha bar that maintains a buzz but never gets too hectic. To feed the mind, Chandra visits Full Circle (5b Khan Market, T 011 2465 5641), a well-stocked bookshop with a rooftop café, while for cultural events, she says nothing beats the India Habitat Centre (see p060).

For full addresses, see Resources.

ARCHITOUR
A GUIDE TO DELHI'S ICONIC BUILDINGS

It's no exaggeration to say that if it weren't for Jawaharlal Nehru, New Delhi would look completely different. Independent India's first prime minister believed the country needed to modernise, but that it should do so within a socialist, pacifist and egalitarian framework. Nehru was especially eager for Delhi to break with its imperial past – both British and Moghul – and he turned to modernism as the solution. His efforts were mostly concentrated in the area running from Chanakyapuri to Mandi House, with Lodi Road as the third side of the triangle, and despite later development, it is still home to some of the best modern architecture in Delhi.

Nehru's love affair with modernism attracted some of the most famous architects of the time. Le Corbusier, Maxwell Fry and Jane Drew, Louis Kahn and Edward D Stone all came to Delhi and left their mark, as did the man who became the city's most prolific resident foreign architect after Lutyens – Joseph Allen Stein. His cluster of buildings in Lodi, including the India International Centre (see p062) and the later India Habitat Centre (see p060), are among the best-loved buildings of that period. Obviously, it wasn't all about foreign influence. From Habib Rahman and Raj Rewal to Shivnath Prasad, AP Kanvinde, Charles Correa and BV Doshi, India's most talented architects have also been and continue to be at the forefront of Delhi's architectural development.
For full addresses, see Resources.

Baha'i House of Worship

The Canadian/Iranian architect Fariborz Sahba's concept for the Baha'i temple in southern Delhi is a combination of the simple and the sublime. The sharp curves of the thin concrete shells that form the structure (overleaf) are reminiscent of Jørn Utzon's Sydney Opera House, but any similarity ends there. Sahba's building, completed in 1986, is a paean to the lotus, a flower held sacred by most Eastern religions. Arranged in three concentric circles and clad in concrete, the shells are conceived as the 'petals', each circle rising higher than the last. The central set of nine petals forms a bud some 40m high, which is open at the top to flood the vast, cathedral-like interior with light. The effect is sufficiently awe-inspiring to silence the noisiest of children.
Kalkaji Park

Baha'i House of Worship

India Habitat Centre
Joseph Allen Stein's 1993 India Habitat
Centre continues to play with some of the
same ideas he first experimented with in
the India International Centre (see p062).
Built with stone, brick and concrete,
Habitat incorporates plenty of green
space and open courtyards, accessed
by towering doorways. Decorative details
are provided by the brickwork itself and
the occasional flourish of turquoise tiles.
Stein brings the gardens into the heart
of his design through a series of soaring,
partially shaded courtyards. So arresting
that they appear to be the real object of
Stein's interest, these courtyards provide
the users of the complex with spaces to
relax, hold informal meetings or simply
to contemplate. Light and airy, there
is nevertheless something institutional
about Habitat, which feels more like a
university campus than a cultural centre.
Lodi Road, T 011 2468 2001

India International Centre

This 1962 complex of buildings, set around two courtyards and within lush gardens, is one of the first commissions completed by Joseph Allen Stein in New Delhi; his Triveni Kala Sangam (T 011 2371 8833) predates it, but wasn't finished until 1977. Built in a style that Stein referred to as 'regional modernism', the India International Centre (IIC) is a mix of local stone, red brick and concrete, with pseudo-Moghul touches, melded with an almost Californian use of space. Although it has been allowed to decay, the IIC retains its warmth and remains a popular destination for the city's intelligentsia. Whether they appreciate the beauty of its covered walkways, delicate filigree claustra and rational, rectilinear angles is doubtful. What is certain is that this low-slung, low-key complex, built on a most human scale, is Stein's Indian masterpiece.
40 Max Mueller Marg, www.iicdelhi.nic.in

Jawahar Vyapar Bhawan

One of the more striking towers on the Janpath, this extravagantly cantilevered building is tall enough to be seen from almost all over Connaught Place. Better known to most visitors as the Central Cottage Industries Emporium – Delhi's impressive, if poorly laid-out pan-Indian handicrafts store – the building's sole nod to its surroundings is the use of red and yellow sandstone, which is positioned in bands across its multiple façades. The octagonal windows, which lend the tower the look of a 1970s multistorey car park, are relatively small and deep-set, helping to keep internal temperatures low.
Janpath, T 011 2332 0439,
www.cottageemporiumindia.com

Secretariat

Three buildings make up the Secretariat complex: the North (above) and South blocks, and Rashtrapati Bhawan. Built on a massive red sandstone plinth, one of few concessions to indigenous architecture, Lutyens' stately centrepiece is essentially an exercise in European classicism, with the occasional Indian embellishment. The 340-room Rashtrapati Bhawan, with its soaring cream-coloured dome, was originally home to the British viceroy, and is now the official residence of the Indian president. The North and South blocks, entrusted to Lutyens' colleague Herbert Baker, are still in daily use, housing the home affairs and finance ministries and the external affairs ministry respectively. *Rajpath*

IGNCA

Established in 1987 as a research centre, the Indira Gandhi National Centre for Arts (IGNCA) was designed by Princeton-based architect Ralph Lerner. Despite its immense size and contemporary look, the relatively unadorned façade, the window design and the use of red and yellow sandstone integrate the building smoothly into the existing urban fabric.
Janpath, www.ignca.nic.in

British Council
Alongside his hulking sandstone-clad
Life Insurance Corporation building, this
is Charles Correa's second contribution
to central Delhi. Completed in 1992, it
is by far the better of the two. A simple
cube, from which segments have been
displaced, it is almost overshadowed by
the looming towers between which it is
squeezed. The façade is enlivened by a
massive, slightly abstract black-on-white
marble mural of a banyan tree, the
work of English painter Howard Hodgkin,
which appears to fall like a shadow across
the various recesses and sharp angles.
Pass through the airy interior to the
rear, where the large courtyard, with its
trailing vines, is dominated by a reflecting
pool behind which hovers the elongated,
androgynous and decidedly mystical
face of Stephen Cox's sculpture of Shiva.
17 Connaught Place, T 011 2371 0717

SHOPPING

THE BEST RETAIL THERAPY AND WHAT TO BUY

There is a simple reason the Moghuls and, after them, the British, lusted after India: its fabulous wealth of treasures, from emeralds the size of eggs to sumptuously embroidered fabrics. But it has been a while since India was the workshop of the world, and much has been lost along the way. More recently, its glittering reputation has been heavily tarnished by its equally exceptional poverty, and its post-Raj socialist fling instilled an insular attitude towards quality – shoddy goods presented as the price for independence.

Although quality remains erratic, production a problem and packaging idiosyncratic, things are changing, and it won't be long before the 'Made in India' label is once again sought after. The country's craft heritage is firmly celebrated in Delhi's shops; the better-quality outlets include the National Crafts Museum Shop (see p080) and the Crafts Council of India's flagship store, Kamala (overleaf), which promotes and works with local artisans.

In fashion, a new generation, led by designers such as Rajesh Pratap Singh (see p082) and Manish Arora (see p078), is setting out to prove that chic doesn't come cheap, that tradition can be modernised and, in Arora's case, that bold colours are nothing to fear. Say goodbye to the tat of the past, swept away by the rising expectations of Delhi's shopping-mad middle class, and prepare to be dazzled by the wares of the world's biggest bazaar.

For full addresses, see Resources.

Bian

Very East Village, Bian's exposed brick and ducts, artfully posed mannequins and subtle lighting are in contrast to the feverish extravaganza that is the branch of Manish Arora next door. The emphasis is very much on Western-style clothing (shirt-dresses, flimsy tops, wraps and jackets with asymmetrical lines), although in a nod to the local market, there are also a few heavily embellished, hand-woven saris, some embroidered with Swarovski crystals. Launched in New York in 2000, Bian is the baby of three sisters, Gurpreet Fleming, Pavan Singh and Harmeet Bajaj, who is one of the co-owners of the Smoke House Grill (see p050). New York-based Fleming designs the clothes, Singh takes care of the manufacturing and Bajaj is responsible for the marketing.
2 Lodi Colony Main Market, T 011 2464 2914

Kamala
The main store of the Crafts Council
of India, whose mission is to 'seek
new markets for traditional artisans',
Kamala sells a rotating range of the
country's more sophisticated artefacts.
The small but well-chosen selection
includes ceramics, textiles and many
pieces with a contemporary aesthetic.
*1 Rajiv Gandhi Handicrafts Bhawan, Baba
Kharak Singh Marg, T 011 6596 9600*

Abraham & Thakore

In a small courtyard on one side of the main building at Lodi Market, this white box of a store, with a single flower floating in a bowl of water at the window, could be the reception area of a luxurious Balinese spa. The palette is subdued – black, white, beige and olive, the universal colours of the global urbanite – but the real joy of these clothes lies in the details: the multicoloured stitching around the buttonholes on a shirt, the colourful splash of appliqué on a tightly wrapped blouse, the fabrics begging to be stroked. If you get the feeling that you've seen these designs somewhere before, it's probably because you have; in addition to its annual show at Maison & Objet in Paris, A&T's clothes are sold at boutiques in New York and Tokyo. *31 Lodi Colony Main Market, T 011 2460 3455, www.abrahamandthakore.com*

Manish Arora Fish Fry
Guaranteed to put a smile on even the
weariest face, this kitsch interior could
be the aftermath of an explosion in a
sweet shop, with sportswear in every
possible colour from cough-drop red
to spearmint ranged against a backdrop
of gods and 1970s Bollywood starlets.
*Shop 7/8, East Bazaar, Garden of
Five Senses, T 011 2953 4785,
www.manisharora.ws*

National Crafts Museum Shop

If you can get past the chaotic layout and damp smell, this shop at the entrance to Charles Correa's National Crafts Museum is well worth a browse. Venture in for a rummage and you will be rewarded with beautiful mirrored Gujarati peasant blouses, some nicely designed handmade paper diaries and photo albums, shapely Hindu statues, colourful jewellery, Tibetan paintings and an admirable selection of coffee-table photobooks. True, most of what is available can be found almost anywhere else in the city, but everything on offer here tends to be of a much higher quality as befits one of the country's crafts showcases. Be warned, though, because it is a government-run shop, the prices are fixed, so bartering won't get you anywhere. The shop is closed on Mondays.

Bhairon Marg, Pragati Maidan,
T 011 2337 1641

Rajesh Pratap Singh

Easy to miss, if only because the sculptural wall of lockers in the entrance suggests a post office rather than a boutique, the interior of Rajesh Pratap Singh's all-white store manages to create maximum impact without ever overshadowing his clothes. A wheeled operating table straight from the Great War, complete with surgical light overhead, bears some of his highlights; the rest are arranged simply on stretchers and rails. Singh designs for both men and women, and eschews the lucrative wedding-sari trade, a staple of many Indian designers. The ambience may shout 'hospital', but there is nothing clinical about these clothes, which are elegant and beautifully tailored. The emphasis is firmly on the cut, hang and texture rather than the colour, which is, for the most part, a palette of monochromes and muted tones.
9 Lodi Colony Main Market,
T 011 3262 4722, www.pratap.ws

Rickshaw Recycle

Loath to throw away the leftovers from their paper-manufacturing business, the folks at Xylem Papercraft decided to recycle it all instead. The result is a playful approach to preserving each piece's former identity, while giving it a new use. Hence placemats woven from folded strips of newspaper (a technique also used to decorate the store) and notebooks bound in the pages of old textbooks and discarded drawings from nursery-school art classes. The ultimate homage to the Indian art of recycling is the small selection of old Bollywood posters. Artfully cropped and framed, they verge on pop-art pastiche.
East Bazaar, Garden of Five Senses,
T 011 3248 5734

Forest Essentials

Until a few years ago, visitors who came to India with notions of organic lotions would leave with suitcases packed full of tchotchkes but light on quality spa goods. Forest Essentials, opened in 2000 by Mira Kulkarni, has changed all that. Simply packaged and created in consultation with Ayurvedic physicians, the first line of soaps has grown into an entire range of beauty products made from organic ingredients. Give yourself a lift with the Kashmiri walnut facial scrub, treat yourself to a bath scented with Madurai jasmine, or shower with a bar of sandalwood and vetiver soap – so deliciously scented that total strangers will be tempted to take a bite. Better yet, buy one of the edible luxury soaps and take a bite for yourself. *46b Khan Market, T 011 4175 7057, www.forestessentialsindia.com*

Sharma Farm
This sprawling series of dusty warehouses
on the outskirts of the city is home to
a mixture of the fake and the fabulous.
A combination of reclamation yard, antique
store and factory, Sharma Farm has been
providing architects, savvy foreign
residents and nostalgic Indian expats with
every conceivable historical household
artefact for more than 30 years. Although
there are literally thousands of objects,
staff will immediately tell you what is new
and what is not. Should you find you've
developed a passion for that elaborately
carved wooden doorway from Gujarat, the
multicoloured scroll stand from a Tibetan
monastery or the delicate red sandstone
filigree balustrade that was once leant
on by some maharaja or another, they
will also be happy to arrange for any
necessary export permits and can ship
your object of desire direct to your door.
Chhatarpur, T 011 2680 7006

SPORTS AND SPAS
WORK OUT, CHILL OUT OR JUST WATCH

Superior sports facilities that do not require membership and a joining fee are rare in Delhi. Gyms exist by the hundreds, but they are old-school establishments where muscled men strain over weights as opposed to body-conscious urbanites struggling with their Nautilus. Most hotel spas, such as at The Oberoi (see p094), admit guests only; however, two recommended independent spas are the women-only Asian Roots (overleaf) and Ozone (D-72 Defence Colony, T 011 4155 0130), which may concede temporary membership. Similarly, pools are in short supply within the city. The few not connected to hotels tend to be outdoors and unheated, and so close between October and May. If your hotel doesn't have its own pool, try the YMCA Tourist Hostel (Jai Singh Marg, T 011 2336 1847), where the facilities can be used on a day-to-day basis.

Of course, India's national sporting obsession is cricket, and if you're lucky enough to be in Delhi when there's a Test match on, don't miss spending a day among the fanatical supporters at the Feroz Shah Kotla stadium (Bahadur Shah Zafar Marg, T 011 2331 9323). For something rather different, Himalayan River Runners (N8 Green Park Main, T 011 2685 2602) can arrange whitewater tours to Rishikesh, five hours north of Delhi, while a class in Laughter Yoga (162 Rameshwar Nagar, Azadpur, T 011 2767 5690) will teach you the manifold benefits of a daily side-splitter.
For full addresses, see Resources.

DDA Sports Complex

Built for the 1982 Asian Games, this lavish, superbly laid out, verdant complex is a sport lover's paradise. There's a beautiful Olympic-sized outdoor pool with diving boards and spectators' stands (in case you have brought your fans), archery, shooting and golf-driving ranges, squash, badminton and tennis courts, football pitches, yoga and aerobics classes – all for £1.30 a day. Designed by one of India's foremost architects, Raj Rewal, the faintly organic forms of the low-rise concrete buildings look like something out of the late 1960s – the massive Chupa-Chups-esque observation tower is particularly *Jetsons* retro. Like many sports complexes in the city, it's currently being smartened up for the 2010 Commonwealth Games.
Siri Fort Marg, T 011 2649 6657, www.dda.org.in

Asian Roots

Kamayani Kanwar's hugely popular spa, fitness centre and beauty salon is the sole women-only establishment of its kind in town. This peaceful retreat on a blindingly busy intersection in Lodi blends European, Indian, Japanese and South-East Asian techniques, all of which are administered by a team of Balinese masseuses. Spacious and light-filled, the spa offers La Prairie treatments, facials and a dizzying array of massage and body scrubs. The Holistic Body Treatment with Hot Stone Therapy is especially popular, but for something a little more exotic, try the Caviar Body Treatment. The fitness centre has all the usual machines and offers yoga classes as well. Lots of locals pop into the hair and beauty salon on the premises.
B5/15 Safdarjung Enclave, T 011 4165 2576, www.myasianroots.com

Lodi Garden

This is one of the most beautiful of Delhi's parks, and its cool, leafy pathways are among the best jogging trails in town. Laid out in 1936, when the village that existed here was relocated, the garden was landscaped in 1968 by Joseph Allen Stein and Garrett Eckbo, and is dotted with the stunning 15th- and 16th-century tombs of the Lodi and Sayyid sultans.
Lodi Road

The Oberoi Spa

Strictly speaking, The Oberoi Spa shouldn't make this list as it is solely for the use of hotel guests or those prepared to book a room on a day-use basis. The reason it is included is purely visual. Of all Delhi's spas, this one is easily the most arresting. Clean, contemporary and ultra-stylish, it is the work of UK-based designers Virgile and Stone and is operated by the Thai chain, Banyan Tree Resorts. The low-lit indoor pool, with its rough-textured columns and raised infinity pool, is a real marvel – the perfect, calming ambience for a soak at the end of a long day. Any kinks that can't be removed with a few laps can be taken care of in the treatment rooms, where the all-Balinese staff offer everything from Jet Lag Massage and Ayurvedic body scrubs to Vichy shower treatments and deep-tissue manipulation.
The Oberoi, Dr Zakir Hussain Marg,
T 011 2436 3030, www.oberoidelhi.com

ESCAPES

WHERE TO GO IF YOU WANT TO LEAVE TOWN

For centuries, Delhi's rulers and their subjects, stuck with a climate that would make the Devil give thanks for his eternity in hell, have retreated to cooler climes each summer. For the Moghuls, this meant relocating to their pleasure gardens on Srinagar's Lake Dal, 10 days' journey away in the Vale of Kashmir. The British opted to stay closer to home – each summer they moved their capital, lock, stock and barrel, to Shimla, a town two days' journey to the north nestled in the Himalayan foothills. Nowadays, the proliferation of budget airlines allows contemporary Delhi-ites to do much the same, albeit with far less bother. Srinagar is 90 minutes away by plane, Shimla about the same by chartered helicopter, while the seaside resorts in places like Goa, Kerala and even the Andamans are now all possible weekend getaways.

Tempting as it may be to leave Delhi's heat and dust for a weekend on the beach or a stroll through Himalayan pine forests, there are also a number of fascinating destinations within easier striking distance. Tiger-spotting at Corbett National Park (Dhikala, T 011 2794 8870), 300km from Delhi, for example, or shopping for jewellery in Jaipur, 260km away, with lunch at the fabulous Rambagh Palace (Bhawani Singh Road, T 014 1221 1919) as an extra treat. They certainly won't offer much respite from the sun, but the trips listed here are worth their weight in perspiration.
For full addresses, see Resources.

Fatehpur Sikri and Agra, Uttar Pradesh

This red-stone city, around 200km from Delhi, was built by the emperor Akbar in 1571, but abandoned 14 years later when the wells ran dry. Akbar had a deep respect for other religions and organised legendary inter-faith discussions. A synthesis of Hindu, Jain and Islamic styles, Fatehpur Sikri is part of that dialogue and has been a source of inspiration for many architects, including Lutyens and BV Doshi. Ninety minutes away is Agra. Make your first stop the glamorous Oberoi Amarvilas (T 056 2223 1515), where you should have lunch or consider spending the night. Begin with a drink on the terrace and your first (distant) view of the Taj (overleaf). When you see it up close, take in all the details: the marble inlay on the outer walls, the stone filigree of the balustrades and the play of light and shadow in the central hall.

Taj Mahal, Agra

Chandigarh, Haryana
Designed by Le Corbusier at the behest
of Nehru, Chandigarh, a short flight
north from Delhi, was built to be the
replacement capital for post-partition
Punjab. Nehru wanted a city 'unfettered
by the past' and with Corbu heading
the plan, he certainly got one: ultra-
modern and yes, *radieuse*. Concentrate
your attentions on the Capitol Complex,
including Punjab University (pictured).

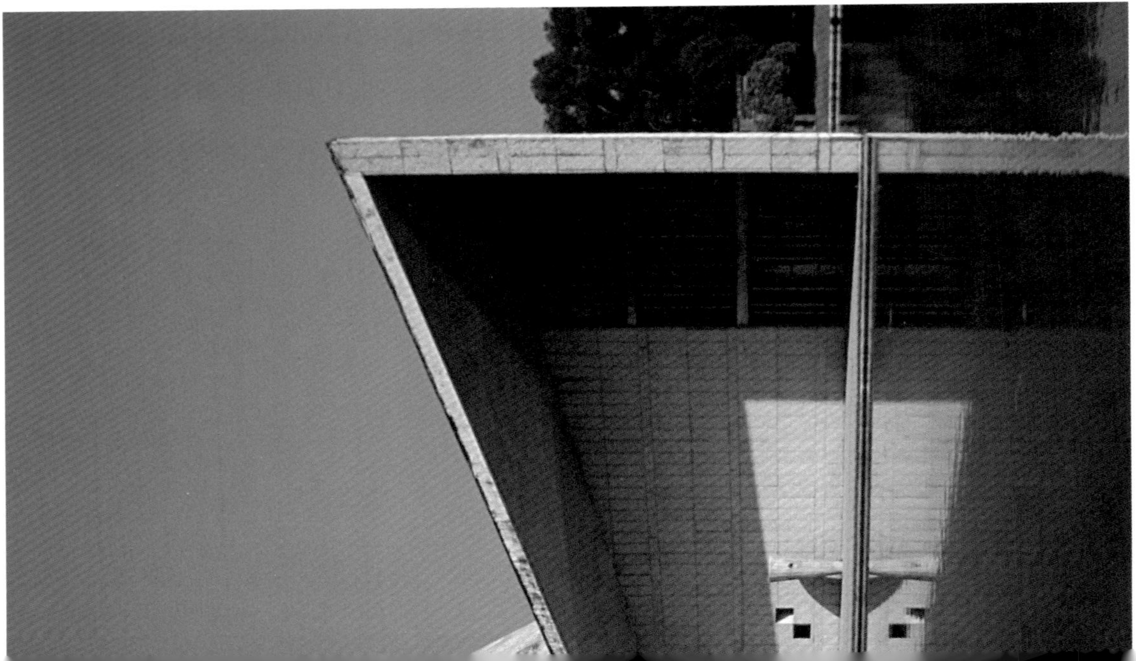

Neemrana Fort-Palace, Rajasthan
At the end of a sometimes juddering, often gritty journey that will take the better part of four hours, the Neemrana Fort-Palace hotel looms abruptly into view. The sprawling 10-level complex, perched on a hilltop just high enough to allow it to dominate the surrounding plains, was built in 1464, and is one of the oldest heritage hotels in India. Services, though, are thoroughly 21st century. The rooms are, for the most part, exquisitely furnished with a mixture of antiques, both Indian and colonial, although some are a tad on the spartan side. If lounging by the pool or in the jacuzzi becomes too much of a chore, consider an Ayurvedic massage, a spot of yoga or the library, stocked with titles straight out of the Raj.
Alwar District, T 014 9424 6006, www.neemranahotels.com

NOTES

SKETCHES AND MEMOS

RESOURCES

CITY GUIDE DIRECTORY

HOTELS

ADDRESSES AND ROOM RATES

The Claridges 017
Room rates:
double, from INR15,000;
Deluxe Room, INR16,500
12 Aurangzeb Marg
T 011 4133 5133
www.claridges-hotels.com

The Imperial 026
Room rates:
double, from INR27,500;
Royal Imperial Suite, from INR70,000
Janpath
T 011 2334 1234
www.theimperialindia.com

Lutyens Bungalow 030
Room rates:
double, INR5,500;
Room 1, INR5,500
39 Prithviraj Road
011 2461 1341
www.lutyensbungalow.co.in

Maidens Hotel 022
Room rates:
double, from INR10,000;
Luxury Suite, INR18,000
7 Sham Nath Marg
T 011 2397 5464
www.maidenshotel.com

Neemrana Fort-Palace 102
Room rates:
double, from INR3,500
Alwar District
Rajasthan
T 014 9424 6006
www.neemranahotels.com

The Oberoi 020
Room rates:
double, from INR15,000;
Kohinoor Suite, from INR200,000
Dr Zakir Hussain Marg
T 011 2436 3030
www.oberoidelhi.com

The Oberoi Amarvilas 097
Room rates:
double, from INR29,500
Taj East Gate Road
Agra
T 056 2223 1515
www.oberoiamarvilas.com

The Park 023
Room rates:
double, from INR16,000;
Residence Suite, from INR18,000;
Presidential Suite, INR50,000
15 Parliament Street
T 011 2374 3000
newdelhi.theparkhotels.com

Rambagh Palace 096
Room rates:
double, from INR40,000
Bhawani Singh Road
Jaipur
T 014 1221 1919
www.tajhotels.com

Trident Hilton 028
Room rates:
double, from INR17,000
443 Udyog Vihar
Gurgaon
T 012 4245 0505
www.trident-hilton.com

WALLPAPER* CITY GUIDES

Editorial Director
Richard Cook

Art Director
Loran Stosskopf
City Editor
Warren Singh-Bartlett
Editor
Rachael Moloney
Executive
Managing Editor
Jessica Firmin
Travel Bookings Editor
Sara Henrichs

Chief Designer
Daniel Shrimpton
Designer
Lara Collins
Map Illustrator
Russell Bell

Photography Editor
Christopher Lands
Photography Assistant
Robin Key

Chief Sub-Editor
Jeremy Case
Sub-Editors
Vicky McGinlay
Stephen Patience
Editorial Assistant
Ella Marshall

Interns
Nicky Ashwell
Rosa Bertoli

Wallpaper* Group
Editor-in-Chief
Tony Chambers
Publisher
Neil Sumner

Contributors
Puru Das
Brian DeMuro
Priya Kishore
Meirion Pritchard
Ellie Stathaki

Wallpaper* ® is a
registered trademark
of IPC Media Limited

All prices are correct at
time of going to press,
but are subject to change.

PHAIDON

Phaidon Press Limited
Regent's Wharf
All Saints Street
London N1 9PA

Phaidon Press Inc
180 Varick Street
New York, NY 10014

Phaidon® is a registered
trademark of Phaidon
Press Limited

www.phaidon.com

First published 2008
© 2008 IPC Media Limited

ISBN 978 0 7148 4739 9

A CIP Catalogue record for
this book is available from
the British Library.

Printed in China

PHOTOGRAPHERS

Manoj Adhikari
Delhi city view, inside
front cover

Clare Arni
Jantar Mantar, pp010-011
The Claridges, p017
The Oberoi, pp020-021
The Park, p023, pp024-025
Lutyens Bungalow,
pp030-031
Raj Ghat, p033
Veda, pp036-037
Nature Morte, p038
Agni, p041
Travertino, pp042-043
Jade, p044
Olive Beach, p045
Ploof!, p046
Magique, p047
Fire, pp048-049
Smoke House Grill, p050
Aura, p051
Ivy, pp052-053
India Habitat Centre,
pp060-061
India International Centre,
pp062-063
Jawahar Vyapar Bhawan,
pp064-065
IGNCA, pp068-069
Bian, p073
Kamala, pp074-075
Abraham & Thakore,
pp076-077

Manish Arora Fish Fry,
pp078-079
National Crafts Museum
Shop, pp080-081
Rajesh Pratap Singh,
pp082-083
Rickshaw Recycle, p084
Forest Essentials, p085
Sharma Farm, pp086-087
DDA Sports Complex, p089
Asian Roots, pp090-091
Lodi Garden, pp092-093
The Oberoi Spa,
pp094-095

Elvele Images/Alamy
Qutab Minar, p012

fnoxx.de
Baha'i House of Worship,
p057, pp058-059

Terje Lillehaug/Alamy
Jama Masjid, pp014-015

Nikreates/Alamy
Fatehpur Sikri and Agra,
Uttar Pradesh, p097

Okapia KG, Germany
India Gate, p013

Tom Pietrasik
Aparna Chandra, p055

Dirk Renckhoff
Chandigarh, Haryana,
pp100-101

Ross Pictures/Corbis
Red Fort, pp034-035

Jacob Silberberg
Taj Mahal, Agra, pp098-099

Paul Springett/Alamy
Secretariat, pp066-067

View Pictures/Alamy
Threesixty°, p039

DELHI

A COLOUR-CODED GUIDE TO THE HOT 'HOODS

OLD DELHI
Moghul monuments and bustling markets jostle for attention in the old walled city

CONNAUGHT PLACE
Shop for Indian handicrafts or visit the giant observatory among Delhi's few high-rises

INDIA GATE
The spectacular heart of Sir Edwin Lutyens' New Delhi packs an architectural punch

CHANAKYAPURI
A wealth of mid-century modern buildings line the leafy avenues of this embassy district

LODI AND NIZAMUDDIN
Find modernism and mosques, wealth and poverty side by side in these two districts

SOUTH DELHI
The new mercantile quarter is where to head for the city's hottest shops and restaurants

For a full description of each neighbourhood, see the Introduction.
Featured venues are colour-coded, according to the district in which they are located.